DATE	NAME	COMPA		UT

DATE	NAME	COMPANY	TIME IN / OUT	

DATE	NAME	COMPANY	TIME IN / OUT	

DATE	NAME	COMPANY	TIME IN / OUT	

DATE	NAME	COMPANY	TIME IN / OUT	

DATE	NAME	COMPANY	TIME IN / OUT	

DATE	NAME	COMPANY	TIME IN / OUT	

DATE	NAME	COMPANY	TIME IN / OUT	

DATE	NAME	COMPANY	TIME IN / OUT	

DATE	NAME	COMPANY	TIME IN / OUT	

DATE	NAME	COMPANY	TIME IN / OUT	

DATE	NAME	COMPANY	TIME IN / OUT	

DATE	NAME	COMPANY	TIME IN / OUT	

DATE	NAME	COMPANY	TIME IN / OUT	

DATE	NAME	COMPANY	TIME IN	/ OUT

DATE	NAME	COMPANY	TIME IN / OUT	

DATE	NAME	COMPANY	TIME IN / OUT	

DATE	NAME	COMPANY	TIME IN / OUT	

DATE	NAME	COMPANY	TIME IN / OUT	

DATE	NAME	COMPANY	TIME IN / OUT	

DATE	NAME	COMPANY	TIME IN / OUT	

DATE	NAME	COMPANY	TIME IN	OUT

DATE	NAME	COMPANY	TIME IN / OUT	

DATE	NAME	COMPANY	TIME IN / OUT	

DATE	NAME	COMPANY	TIME IN / OUT	

DATE	NAME	COMPANY	TIME IN / OUT	

DATE	NAME	COMPANY	TIME IN / OUT	

DATE	NAME	COMPANY	TIME IN / OUT	

DATE	NAME	COMPANY	TIME IN / OUT	

DATE	NAME	COMPANY	TIME IN / OUT	

DATE	NAME	COMPANY	TIME IN / OUT	

DATE	NAME	COMPANY	TIME IN / OUT	

DATE	NAME	COMPANY	TIME IN / OUT	

DATE	NAME	COMPANY	TIME IN / OUT	

DATE	NAME	COMPANY	TIME IN / OUT	

DATE	NAME	COMPANY	TIME IN / OUT	

DATE	NAME	COMPANY	TIME IN / OUT	

DATE	NAME	COMPANY	TIME IN / OUT	

DATE	NAME	COMPANY	TIME IN / OUT	

DATE	NAME	COMPANY	TIME IN / OUT	

DATE	NAME	COMPANY	TIME IN / OUT	

DATE	NAME	COMPANY	TIME IN / OUT	

DATE	NAME	COMPANY	TIME IN / OUT	

DATE	NAME	COMPANY	TIME IN / OUT	

DATE	NAME	COMPANY	TIME IN / OUT	

DATE	NAME	COMPANY	TIME IN / OUT	

DATE	NAME	COMPANY	TIME IN / OUT	

DATE	NAME	COMPANY	TIME IN / OUT	

DATE	NAME	COMPANY	TIME IN / OUT	

DATE	NAME	COMPANY	TIME IN / OUT	

DATE	NAME	COMPANY	TIME IN / OUT	

DATE	NAME	COMPANY	TIME IN / OUT	

DATE	NAME	COMPANY	TIME IN / OUT	

DATE	NAME	COMPANY	TIME IN / OUT	

DATE	NAME	COMPANY	TIME IN / OUT	

DATE	NAME	COMPANY	TIME IN / OUT	

DATE	NAME	COMPANY	TIME IN / OUT	

DATE	NAME	COMPANY	TIME IN / OUT	

DATE	NAME	COMPANY	TIME IN / OUT	

DATE	NAME	COMPANY	TIME IN / OUT	

DATE	NAME	COMPANY	TIME IN / OUT	

DATE	NAME	COMPANY	TIME IN / OUT	

DATE	NAME	COMPANY	TIME IN / OUT	

DATE	NAME	COMPANY	TIME IN / OUT	

DATE	NAME	COMPANY	TIME IN / OUT	

DATE	NAME	COMPANY	TIME IN / OUT	

DATE	NAME	COMPANY	TIME IN / OUT	

DATE	NAME	COMPANY	TIME IN / OUT	

DATE	NAME	COMPANY	TIME IN / OUT	

DATE	NAME	COMPANY	TIME IN / OUT	

DATE	NAME	COMPANY	TIME IN / OUT	

DATE	NAME	COMPANY	TIME IN / OUT	

DATE	NAME	COMPANY	TIME IN / OUT	

DATE	NAME	COMPANY	TIME IN / OUT	

DATE	NAME	COMPANY	TIME IN / OUT	

DATE	NAME	COMPANY	TIME IN / OUT	

DATE	NAME	COMPANY	TIME IN / OUT	

DATE	NAME	COMPANY	TIME IN / OUT	

DATE	NAME	COMPANY	TIME IN / OUT	

DATE	NAME	COMPANY	TIME IN / OUT	

DATE	NAME	COMPANY	TIME IN / OUT	

DATE	NAME	COMPANY	TIME IN / OUT	

DATE	NAME	COMPANY	TIME IN / OUT	

DATE	NAME	COMPANY	TIME IN / OUT	

DATE	NAME	COMPANY	TIME IN / OUT	

DATE	NAME	COMPANY	TIME IN / OUT	

DATE	NAME	COMPANY	TIME IN / OUT	

DATE	NAME	COMPANY	TIME IN / OUT	

DATE	NAME	COMPANY	TIME IN / OUT	

DATE	NAME	COMPANY	TIME IN / OUT	

DATE	NAME	COMPANY	TIME IN / OUT	

DATE	NAME	COMPANY	TIME IN / OUT	

DATE	NAME	COMPANY	TIME IN / OUT	

DATE	NAME	COMPANY	TIME IN / OUT	

DATE	NAME	COMPANY	TIME IN / OUT	

DATE	NAME	COMPANY	TIME IN / OUT	

DATE	NAME	COMPANY	TIME IN / OUT	

DATE	NAME	COMPANY	TIME IN / OUT	

DATE	NAME	COMPANY	TIME IN / OUT	

DATE	NAME	COMPANY	TIME IN / OUT	

DATE	NAME	COMPANY	TIME IN / OUT	

DATE	NAME	COMPANY	TIME IN / OUT	

DATE	NAME	COMPANY	TIME IN / OUT	

DATE	NAME	COMPANY	TIME IN / OUT	

DATE	NAME	COMPANY	TIME IN / OUT	

DATE	NAME	COMPANY	TIME IN / OUT	

DATE	NAME	COMPANY	TIME IN / OUT	

DATE	NAME	COMPANY	TIME IN / OUT	

DATE	NAME	COMPANY	TIME IN / OUT	

DATE	NAME	COMPANY	TIME IN / OUT	

DATE	NAME	COMPANY	TIME IN / OUT	

DATE	NAME	COMPANY	TIME IN / OUT	

DATE	NAME	COMPANY	TIME IN / OUT	

DATE	NAME	COMPANY	TIME IN / OUT	

DATE	NAME	COMPANY	TIME IN / OUT	

DATE	NAME	COMPANY	TIME IN / OUT	

DATE	NAME	COMPANY	TIME IN / OUT	

DATE	NAME	COMPANY	TIME IN / OUT	

DATE	NAME	COMPANY	TIME IN / OUT	

DATE	NAME	COMPANY	TIME IN / OUT	

DATE	NAME	COMPANY	TIME IN / OUT	

DATE	NAME	COMPANY	TIME IN / OUT	

DATE	NAME	COMPANY	TIME IN / OUT	

DATE	NAME	COMPANY	TIME IN / OUT	

DATE	NAME	COMPANY	TIME IN / OUT	

DATE	NAME	COMPANY	TIME IN / OUT	

DATE	NAME	COMPANY	TIME IN / OUT	

DATE	NAME	COMPANY	TIME IN / OUT	

DATE	NAME	COMPANY	TIME IN / OUT	

DATE	NAME	COMPANY	TIME IN / OUT	

DATE	NAME	COMPANY	TIME IN / OUT	

DATE	NAME	COMPANY	TIME IN / OUT	

DATE	NAME	COMPANY	TIME IN / OUT	

DATE	NAME	COMPANY	TIME IN / OUT	

DATE	NAME	COMPANY	TIME IN / OUT	

DATE	NAME	COMPANY	TIME IN / OUT	

DATE	NAME	COMPANY	TIME IN / OUT	

DATE	NAME	COMPANY	TIME IN / OUT	

DATE	NAME	COMPANY	TIME IN / OUT	

DATE	NAME	COMPANY	TIME IN / OUT	

DATE	NAME	COMPANY	TIME IN / OUT	

DATE	NAME	COMPANY	TIME IN / OUT	

DATE	NAME	COMPANY	TIME IN / OUT	

DATE	NAME	COMPANY	TIME IN / OUT	

DATE	NAME	COMPANY	TIME IN / OUT	

DATE	NAME	COMPANY	TIME IN / OUT	

DATE	NAME	COMPANY	TIME IN / OUT	

DATE	NAME	COMPANY	TIME IN / OUT	

DATE	NAME	COMPANY	TIME IN / OUT	

DATE	NAME	COMPANY	TIME IN / OUT	

Made in the USA
Monee, IL
12 February 2021

60339284R00088